Something Magic
Mel Atkey and the Musical Theatre

Vocal and Piano Score

FriendlysongMusic

Copyright ©2014 The Friendlysong Company, Inc.

All Rights Reserved. No portion of this book, with the exception of brief extracts for the purpose of literary or scholarly review, may be reproduced in any form without the permission of the publisher.

All song titles: Friendlysong Music (SOCAN)

Published by The Friendlysong Company, Inc.
4827 Georgia Street, Delta, British Columbia, Canada V4K 2T1

Cataloguing:

> Atkey, Mel (1958-)
>
> Something Magic – Mel Atkey and the Musical Theatre
>
> ISBN 978-0-9916957-2-0
>
> 1 - Music – Musical Theatre – Printed music

Cover photos: Top, L-R: Matthew Morse, *O Pioneers!*; Jennifer Lee Jellicorse, Stephen Weller, *Perfect Timing*; Lisa Neubauer, *O Pioneers!*

Bottom, L-R: Kristin Danielle Klabunde, Monica Soyemi, *A Little Princess* (both photos)

Table of Contents

From *O Pioneers!*:

    "Second Chances"

    "Never Fear"

From *A Little Princess*:

    "Keep Up Your Chin"

    "Emily"

    "She's Not a Princess Now"

    "Royal Vaudeville Show"

    "Being Nice"

    "Take Away"

From *Perfect Timing*:

    "When I See Her Eyes"

    "Something in the Air"

    "Miracle"

    "High School Mornings"

    "He Touched Me"

From *Shikara*:

    "Far Away"

    "You Could Have Possibilities"

    "Looking at the World"

From *The Grand Finale*:

    "Something Magic"

    "Another You"

From *I Can Fly My Kite to the Moon*:

    "I Can Fly My Kite to the Moon"

    "He Says He Loves Me"

    "Running Away"

    "Walking on Waterfalls"

    "The Things I'm Holding Inside Me"

From *Amchitka*:

    "Valentine's Day"

    "Once in My Life"

From *Play to Win*:

    "I Frightened Him Away"

    "A Cold Front"

    "The Power of Advertising"

From *Poor Little Rich Girl Sings the Blues*:

    "Picasso"

Misc:

    "Alone on Christmas Eve"

 Mel Atkey has been writing musicals ever since he was in high school in his native Vancouver. He was a finalist for the Musical of the Year competition in Aarhus, Denmark, and his work has been short-listed for the Vivian Ellis Prize, the Quest for New Musicals, the Ken Hill Prize and Musical Stairs. His first musical, *Shikara*, was produced on radio in Canada. A single was released by singer Janice Jaud of one of the songs, "Far Away", and received airplay across Canada and the U.S.

Mel Atkey began his career in 1977 by co-producing a jazz concert with Vancouver impresario Willi Germann. This experience would later be recalled in his musical *Poor Little Rich Girl Sings the Blues*. Other early projects included a telethon featuring folk singer Tom Northcott, and he spent two years as a theatre critic before moving to Toronto to pursue his career as a musical theatre writer. He was commissioned to write songs for CBC Radio, and was a member of the Guild of Canadian Musical Theatre Writers' Lehman Engel Workshop. He was a director of the Cabaret and Musical Theatre Alliance until he moved to London in 1991. He made his New York debut in April 2001 with an off-off-Broadway showcase of *O Pioneers!* with book by Robert Sickinger. This show was then a finalist for "Stages 2002" at the New Tuners theatre in Chicago. Their second musical, *A Little Princess* was presented at Wings Theatre in New York in 2003, and his two character musical *Perfect Timing*, for which he wrote the book as well as music and lyrics, was showcased to great acclaim as part of Greenwich Theatre (London)'s Musical Futures series. He wrote the opening number for Janie Dee's critically acclaimed one-woman show.

His book *When We Both Got to Heaven* tells the story of his ancestor James Atkey, who came to Georgian Bay from the Isle of Wight in 1854 as a teacher to the Ojibwa. It was published by Natural Heritage Books, Toronto, in October 2002. A second book, *Broadway North: The Dream of a Canadian Musical Theatre was published by Natural Heritage in 2006*. His working follow-up, *A Million Miles from Broadway: Musical Theatre Beyond New York and London* was published in 2012. *Running Away with the Circus – or – "Now Is the Winter of our Missing Tent*, published in 2013, tells of his experience with the big top on tour in Taiwan.

I made my New York debut in 2001 by writing seven songs for Robert Sickinger's adaptation of Willa Cather's 1913 novel *O Pioneers!* presented at Producers Club II in Manhattan. The cast included Matthew Morse as Emil Bergson, Lisa Neubauer as Marie Tovesky and Jennifer Trible as Alexandra Bergson. Musical direction was by Daniel Feyer. Emil and Marie have been friends since childhood. While Emil is secretly in love with Marie, he learns that she has married the short-tempered Frank Shabata, a decision she has begun to regret, but as a firm Catholic she feels bound to stay with him. ("Second Chances") When Frank finds the two of them together, he kills them both. Emil's sister Alexandra finds the strength to forgive Frank. ("Never Fear") (This latter song has since been sung in both churches and cabarets!)

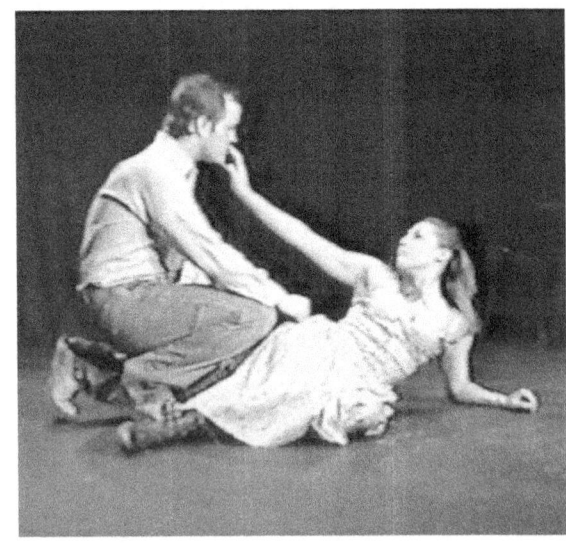

Second Chances

Music and Lyrics by Mel Atkey

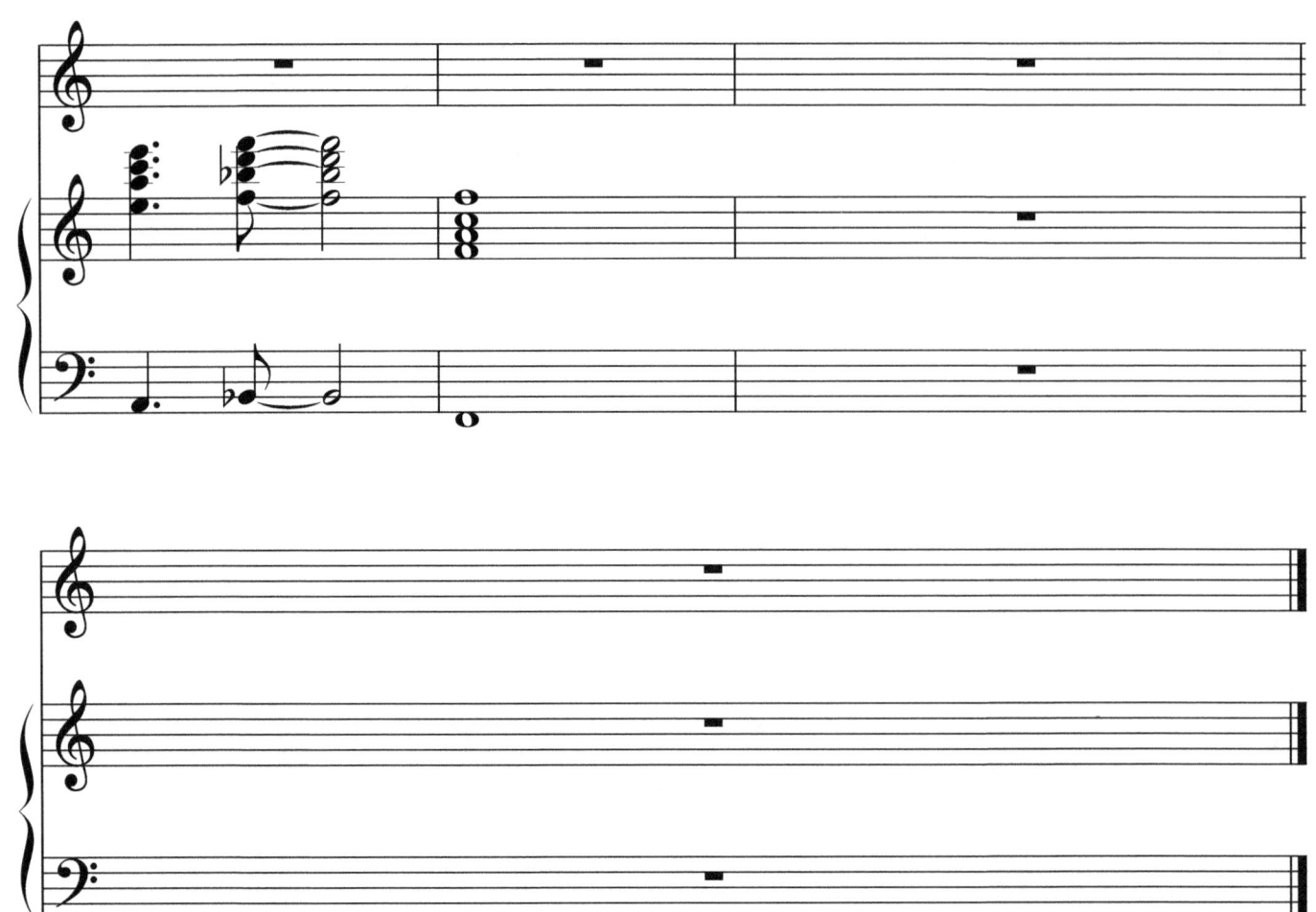

Never Fear

Music and Lyrics by Mel Atkey

© 2001 Mel Atkey All Rights Reserved.

Bob Sickinger and I followed *O Pioneers* with *A Little Princess* in 2003, based on the 1905 children's novel by Frances Hodgson Burnett. presented as a part of Wings Theatre's New Musicals season in their small Greenwich Village theatre. The role of Miss Minchin was played by the late Patty Montano and Colonel Crewe was played by David Lee Kellner, while the part of Sara Crewe was shared by Kristin Danielle Klabunde (who was the last Young Cosette in the original Broadway production of *Les Misérables*) and Grace Cleary. Musical direction was by Mary-Ann Ivan.

"Mel Atkey, who wrote the score and lyrics, has composed lovely music." – *New York Times*, 7 November 2003.

"*A Little Princess*, based on the classic Frances Hodgson Burnett novel, enchants with carefully drawn characters, nicely written songs, and a comfortably old-fashioned feel... The children in the audience loved it, including my daughter Olivia... Mel Atkey's songs were catchy; I heard Olivia humming them during intermission." – *Backstage (New York)*

"The songs, written by Mel Atkey, perfectly match the scenes. A banjo ads authentic American character while stately drum rolls introduce the Colonel. 'Keep Up Your Chin' carries an especially sweet melody and emphasizes the importance of being optimistic." – *Show Business*.

Keep Up Your Chin

Emily

Royal Vaudeville Show

Music and lyrics by Mel Atkey

© 2003 Mel Atkey

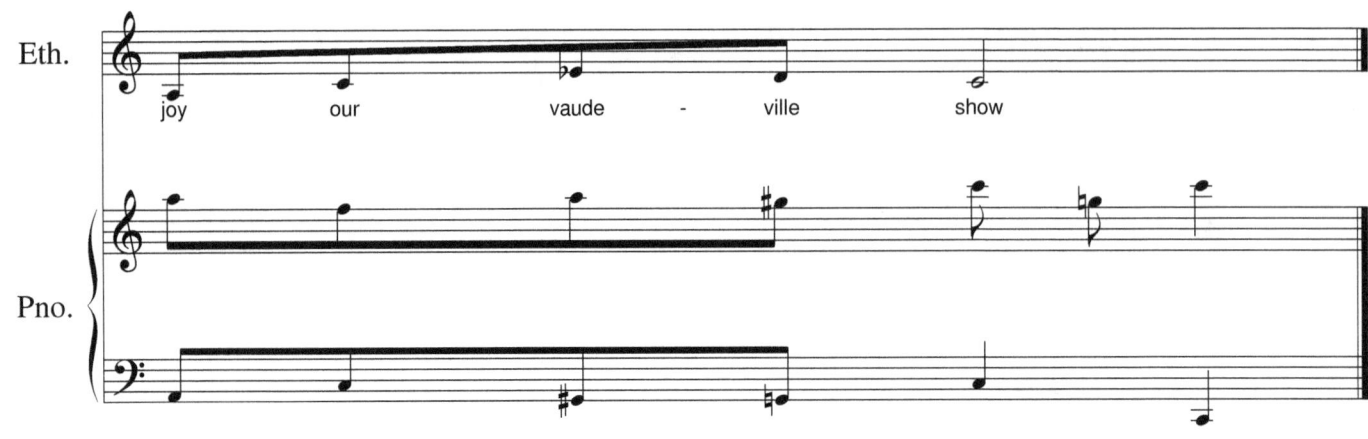

Being Nice

Take Away

Music and Lyrics by Mel Atkey

© 2003 Mel Atkey

Perfect Timing is a two-hander musical that was presented in a heavily abridged version at London's Greenwich Theatre as a part of their Musical Futures season in 2005. This showcase featured Jennifer Lee Jellicorse as "Angela" and Stephen Weller as "Michael", with musical direction by Philip Godfrey. A finalist in the Musical of the Year competition in Aarhus, Denmark, sponsored by DR-TV. "Something in the Air", with special lyrics, was used by English actress Janie Dee as the opening number for her 2004-05 cabaret act.

"Love it. Great songs... Good dialogue, lyrics and excellent composition... Style and finesse about the piece, felt like an established piece of musical theatre... Fantastic. Best new work I've seen in so long – didn't want it to end. Such good lyrics – smart and witty, refreshingly different... Witty, toe tapping tunes... Interesting, unusual and highly amusing" – Audience comments from "Musical Futures" showcase, Greenwich Theatre, London, 2005

When I See Her Eyes

Music and lyrics by Mel Atkey

© 1993 The Friendlysong Company, Inc.

Something In the Air

Music and Lyrics by Mel Atkey

© 1991 The Friendlysong Company, Inc.

Miracle

Music and Lyrics by Mel Atkey

© 1991 The Friendlysong Company, Inc.

High School Mornings

Music and lyrics by Mel Atkey

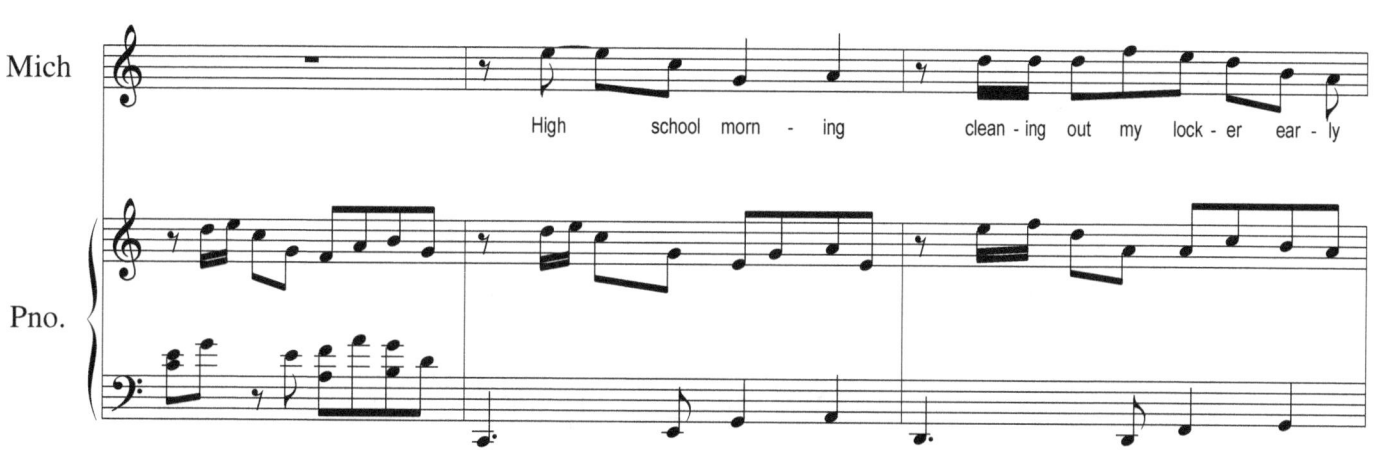

© 2010 The Friendlysong Company, Inc.

He Touched Me

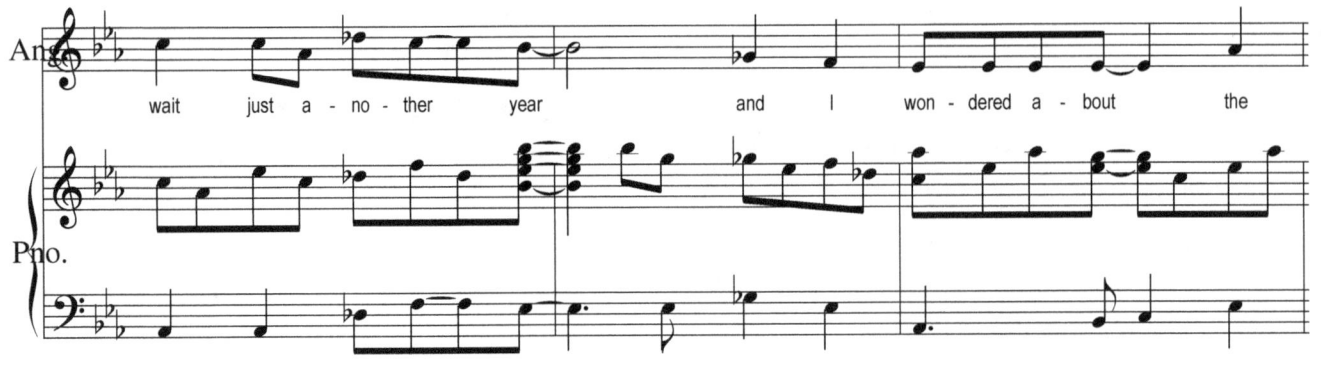

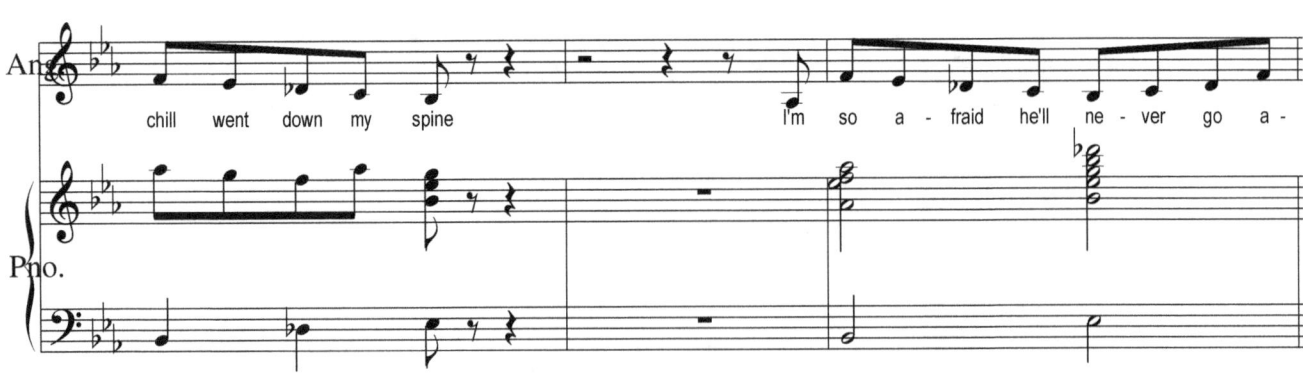

SHIKARA

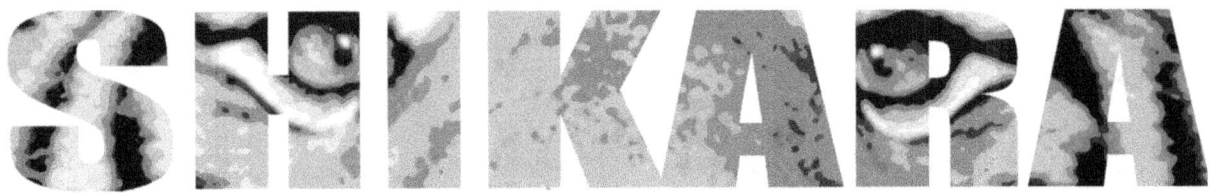

Shikara is my earliest work as a composer. Based on stories my father told me when I was a child about a tiger who was afraid of his own shadow, it has never been produced on stage, although an abridged version was presented on a university radio station in Toronto with Philip Eckman as "Fraidy Cat", Tanya Austin as "Devi", Gerald Smuin as "Madinlal" and Jessica-Snow Wilson as "Davinder". A single was released of the song "Far Away" sung by Janice Jaud in 1980.

"AS A COMPOSER, YOU SHOW ENORMOUS PROMISE— YOU HAVE A WONDERFUL GIFT FOR MELODY, GREAT MUSICALITY, A GOOD SENSE OF HOW TO USE A CHORUS TO MAKE A SONG INTERESTING; IN SHORT, I FEEL YOU HAVE THE POTENTIAL FOR A REAL CAREER AS A THEATRE COMPOSER. LUCKY YOU — SUCH TALENTS ARE RARER THAN YOU KNOW." — STEPHEN SCHWARTZ, COMPOSER OF *GODSPELL*, *THE BAKER'S WIFE*, *PRINCE OF EGYPT* AND *WICKED*.

"IT IS POLISHED AND STYLISH AND KNOWS WHAT IT IS DOING... THIS IS GREAT FUN... I THINK THAT THIS MUSICAL SHOWS HUGE PROMISE... THE MUSIC IS WELL SHAPED AND THE STORY IS HEART RENDING... CLEARLY MEL HAS A GENUINE UNDERSTANDING OF WRITING FOR THE MUSICAL THEATRE."— JUDGES, THE *QUEST FOR NEW MUSICALS*.

Far Away

Music and Lyrics by Mel Atkey

© 1980 The Friendlysong Company, Inc.

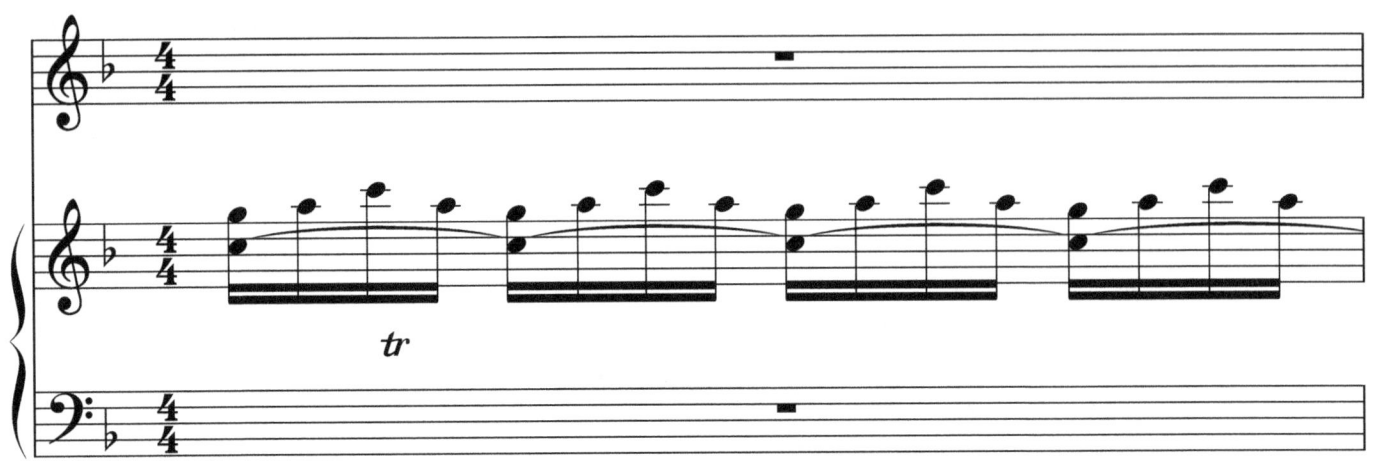

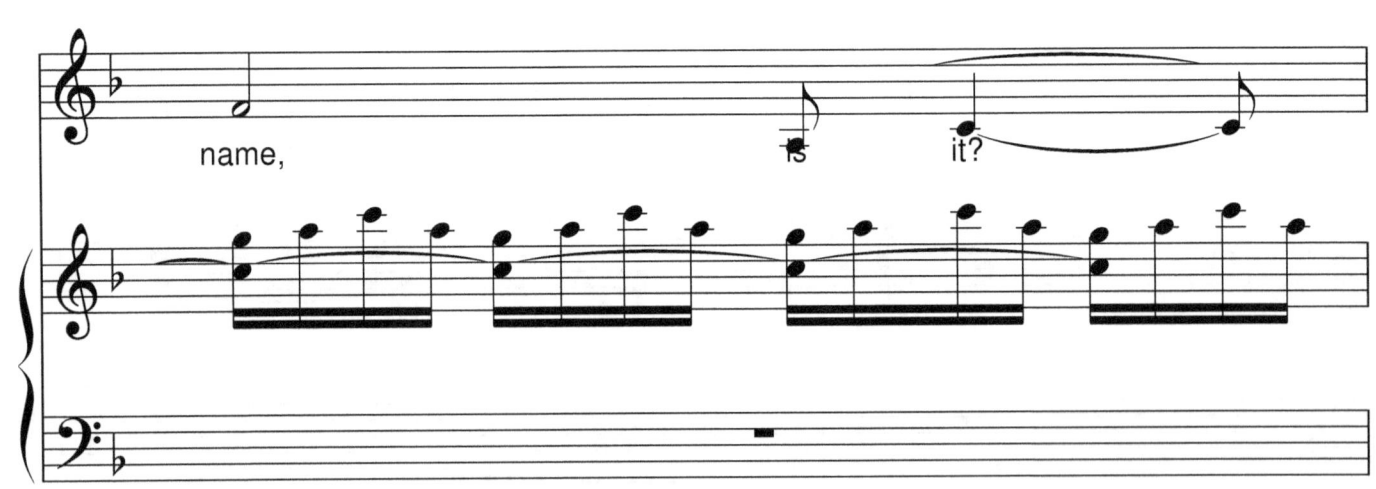

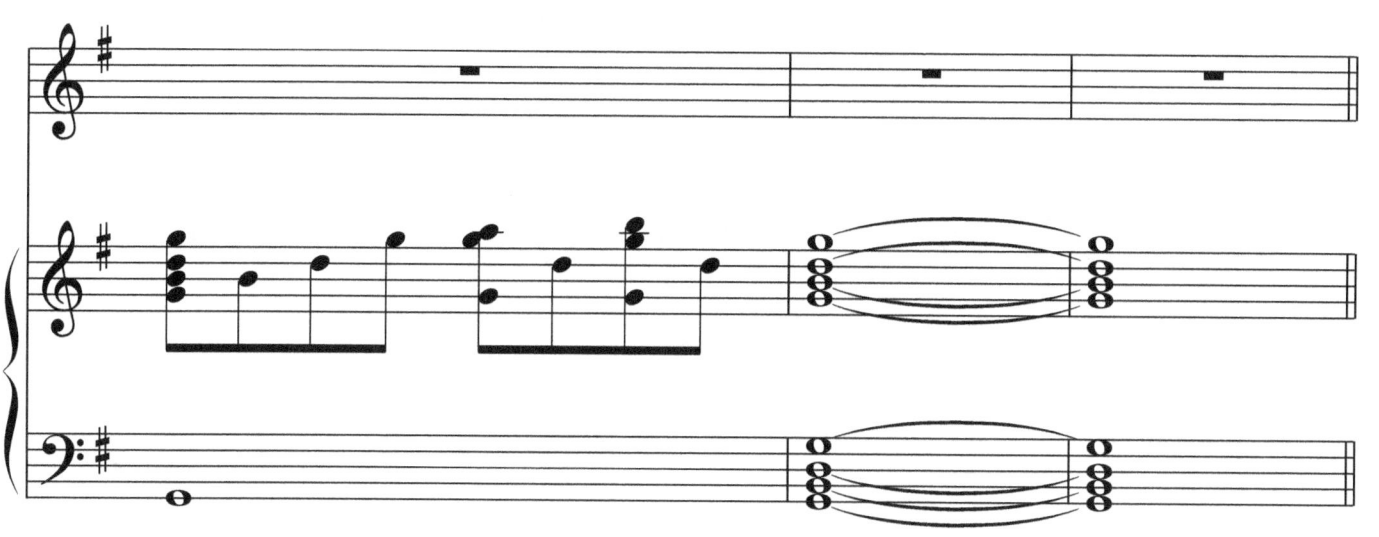

You Could Have Possibilities

Music and lyrics by Mel Atkey

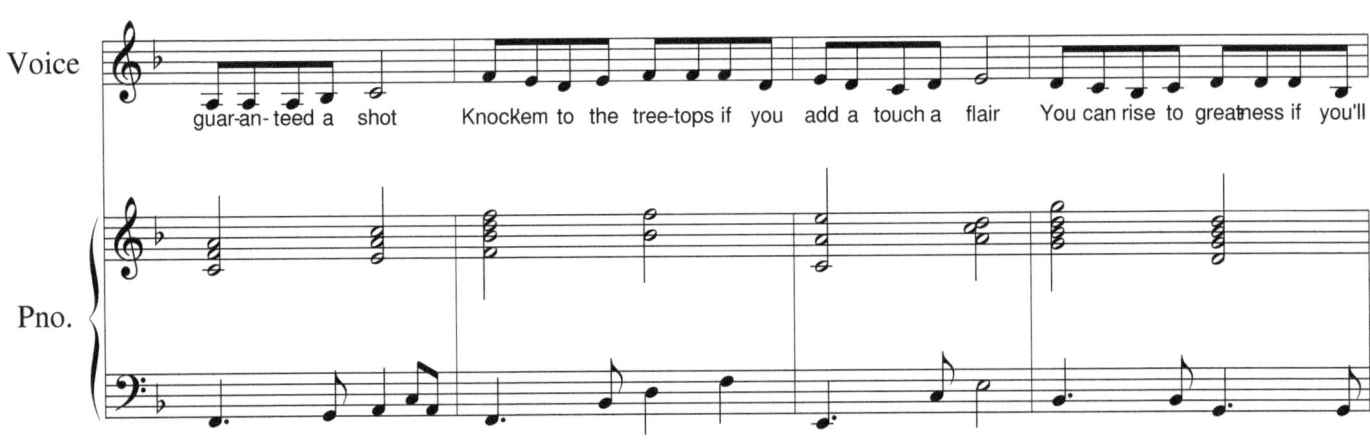

© 2006 The Friendlysong Company, Inc.

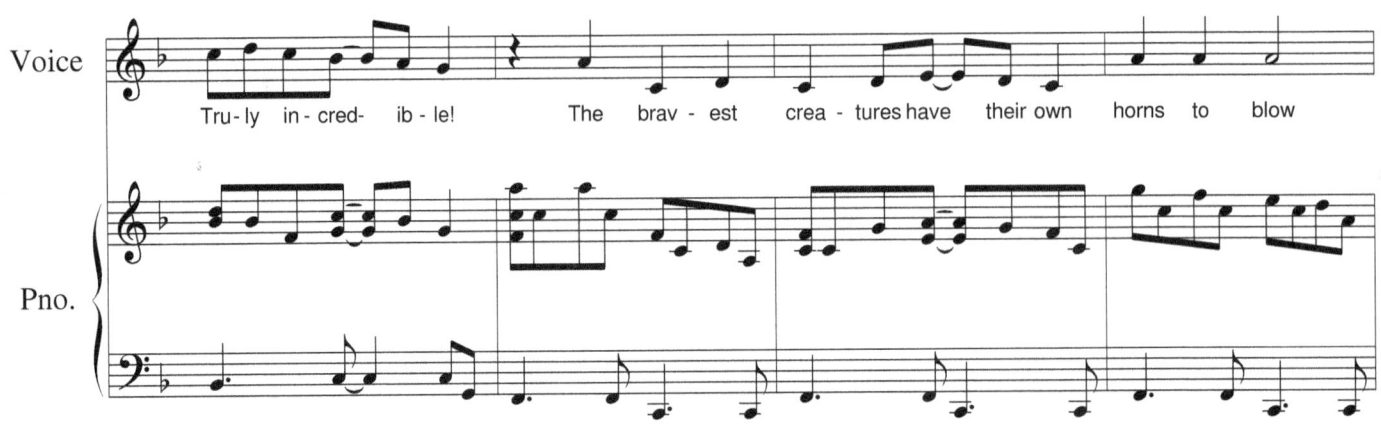

Looking at the World

Music and lyrics by Mel Atkey

© 2006 The Friendlysong Company, Inc.

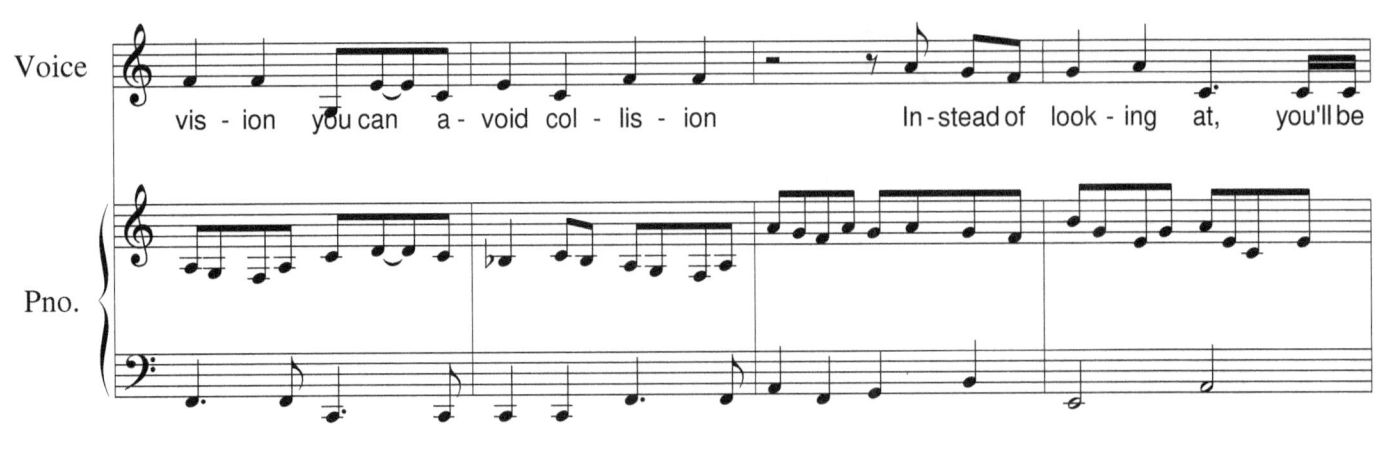

THE GRAND FINALE

Although *The Grand Finale* has never been seen on stage, it was workshopped in Toronto with James Doohan (*Star Trek*'s "Scotty") as an actor auditioning for heaven. The workshop was directed by Richard Ouzounian with piano accompaniment by David Warrack.

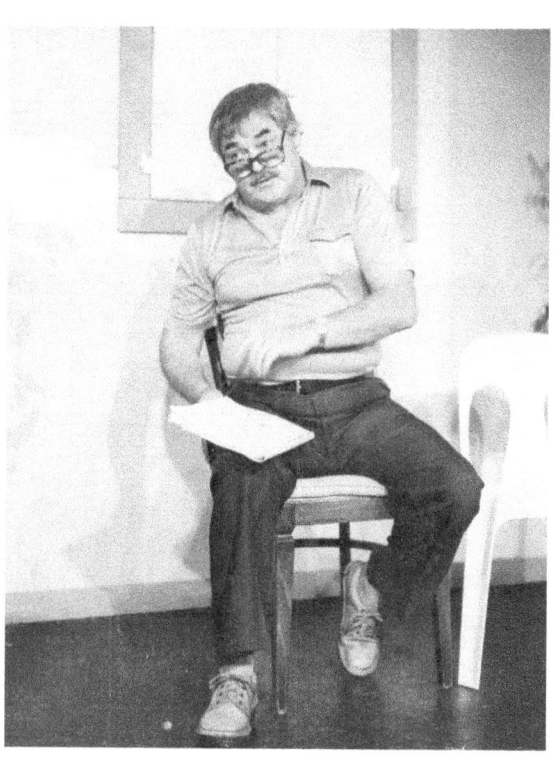

"IT'S ONE OF THOSE THINGS WHERE YOU LAUGH A LOT AND THEN LAUGH SOME MORE, AND THEN YOU FIND OUT THAT YOU'RE CRYING BECAUSE OF WHAT YOU WERE LAUGHING ABOUT." - RICHARD OUZOUNIAN, FORMER ASSOCIATE DIRECTOR OF THE STRATFORD SHAKESPEAREAN FESTIVAL OF CANADA.

"TO ME, *THE GRAND FINALE* IS SUCH A TERRIFIC PLAY. IT'S A CHARACTER THAT I WOULD LOVE TO CREATE." - JAMES DOOHAN

Something Magic

Music and Lyrics by Mel Atkey

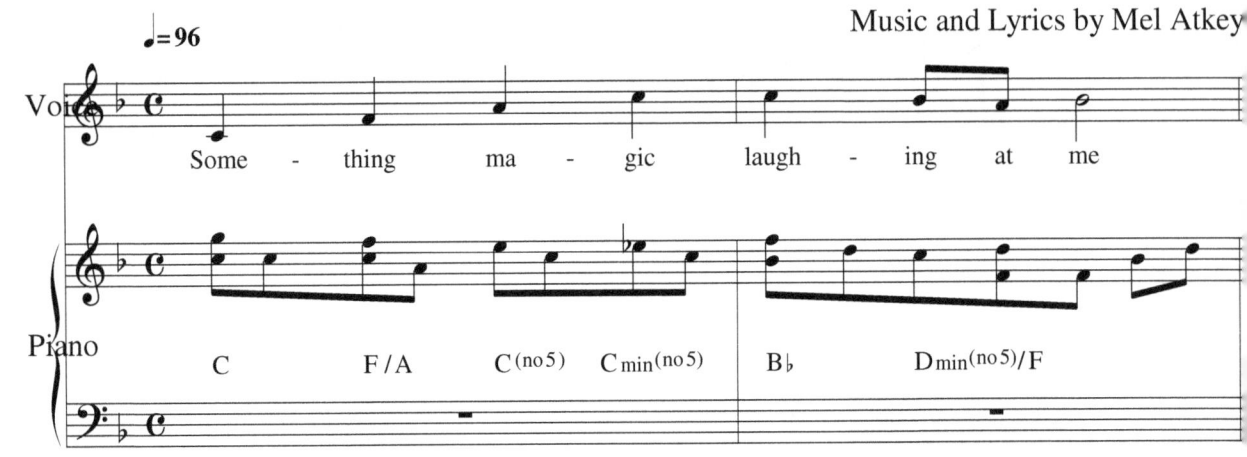

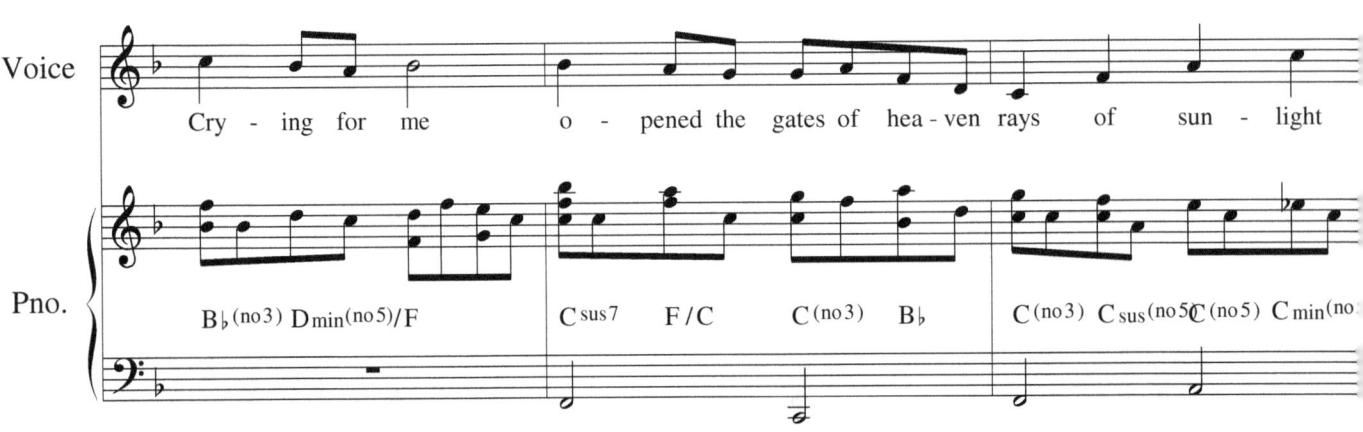

© 1986 The Friendlsyong Company, Inc.

Another You

Instructions

Music and Lyrics by Mel Atkey

© 2013 Friendlysong Music

Unfinished and Unproduced Musicals

The remaining songs are all from unfinished and unproduced musicals, except for "Alone on Christmas Eve", which was intended as a cabaret number. *Amchitka* and *Play to Win* were intended to be "Companion Pieces" for *Perfect Timing*. *Amchitka* being Michael's back story and *Play to Win* Angela's. *Amchitka* is set in a junior high school in Vancouver during a student protest, while *Play to Win* is set in a London advertising agency. (The plot is freely adapted from Carlo Goldoni's 1753 comedy *Mirandolina*. *I Can Fly My Kite to the Moon* tells the story of a boy genius who is tormented by his peers, and escapes into a world of aliens and starships. Only his sister Tessa holds the key to his healing.

I Can Fly My Kite to the Moon

Music and Lyrics by Mel Atkey

©2000 Mel Atkey

He Says He Loves Me

© 2002 Mel Atkey

Running Away

Music and Lyrics by Mel Atkey

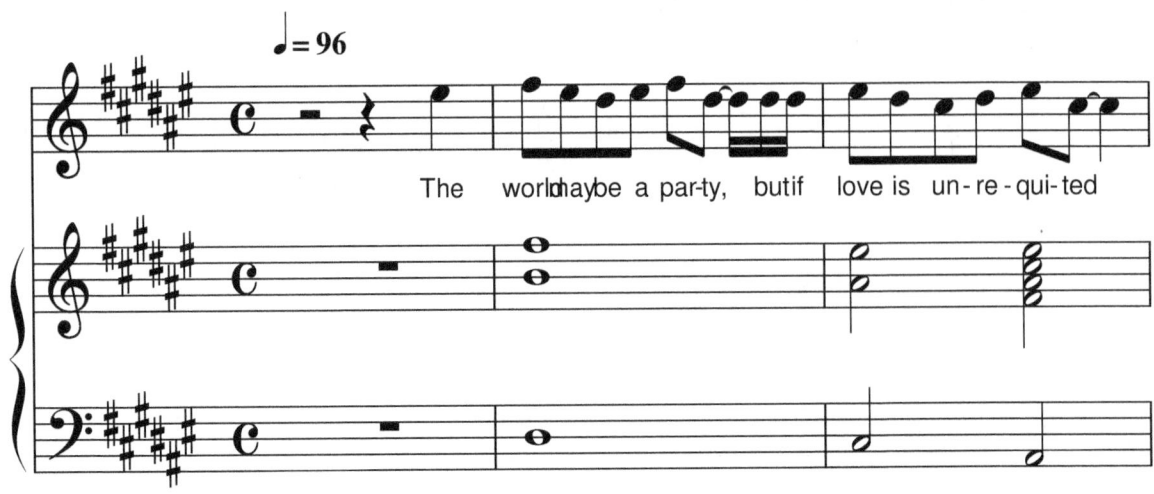

(c) 2000 Mel Atkey

145

Walking on Waterfalls

Music and Lyrics by Mel Atkey

© 1999 Mel Atkey

159

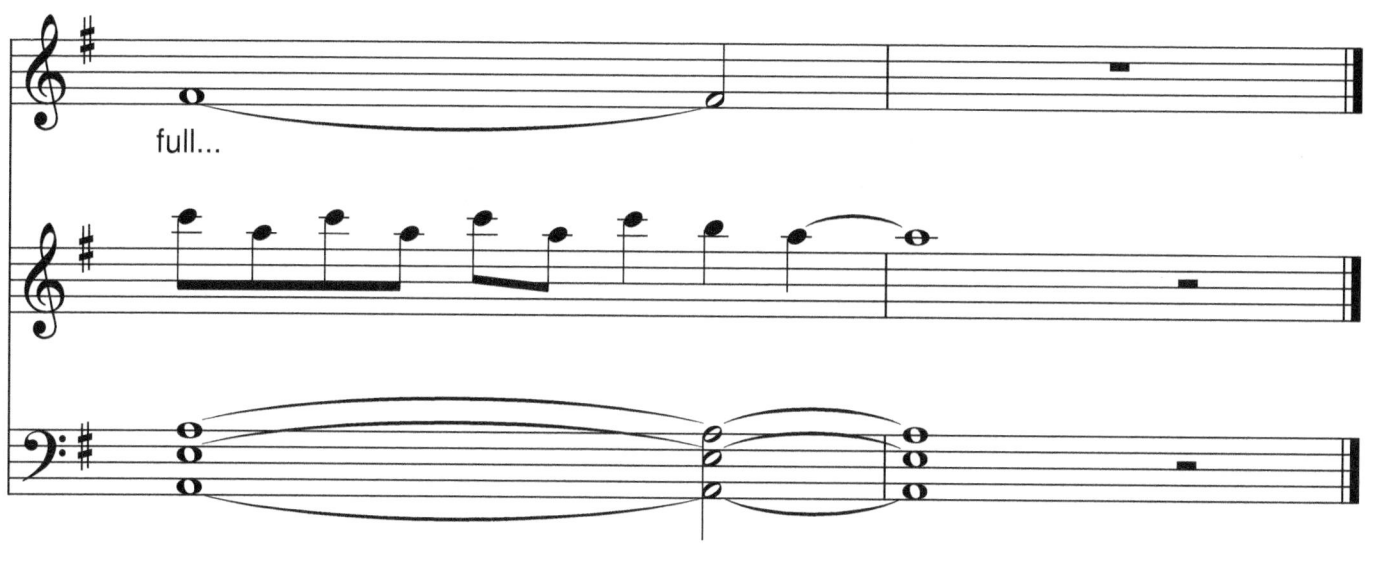

The Things I'm Holding Inside Me

Music and Lyrics by Mel Atkey

© 2000 Mel Atkey

Valentine's Day

Music and Lyrics by Mel Atkey

© 2002 Mel Atkey/The Friendlysong Company, Inc.

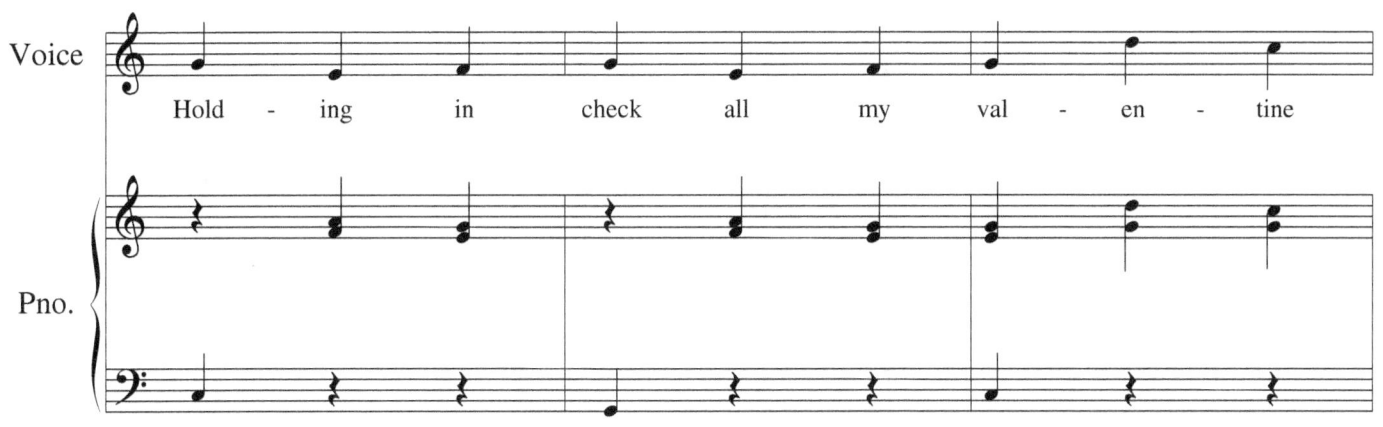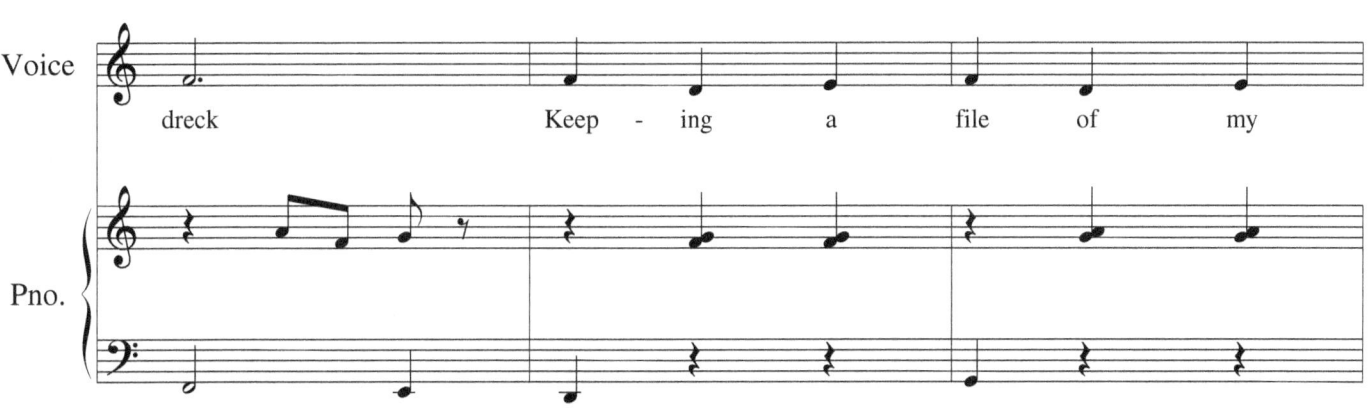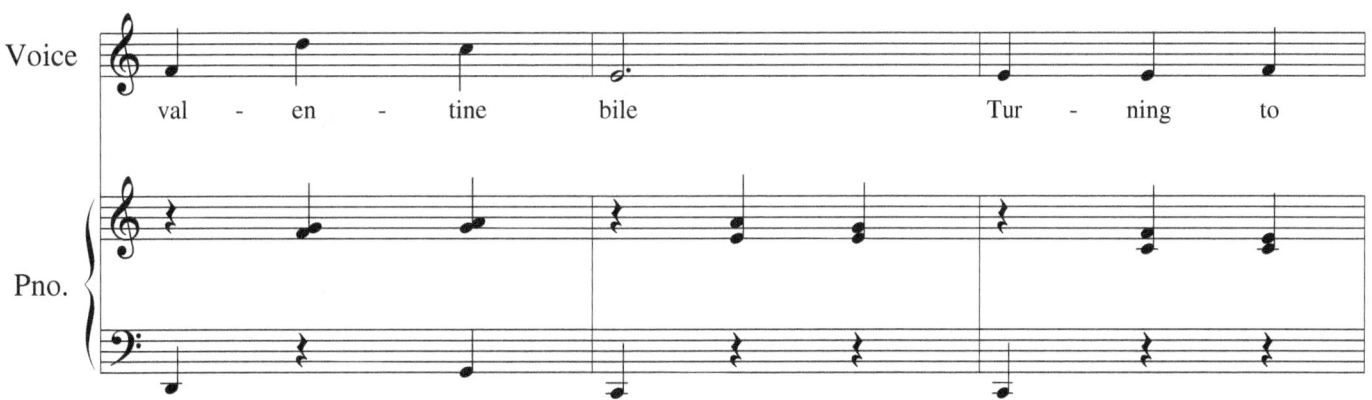

Once In My Life

Music and Lyrics by Mel Atkey

© 2002 Mel Atkey

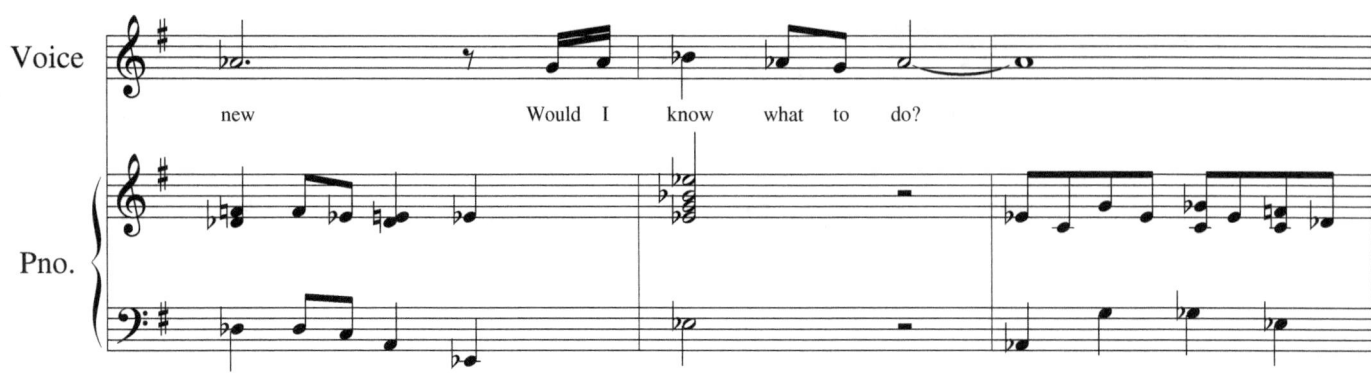
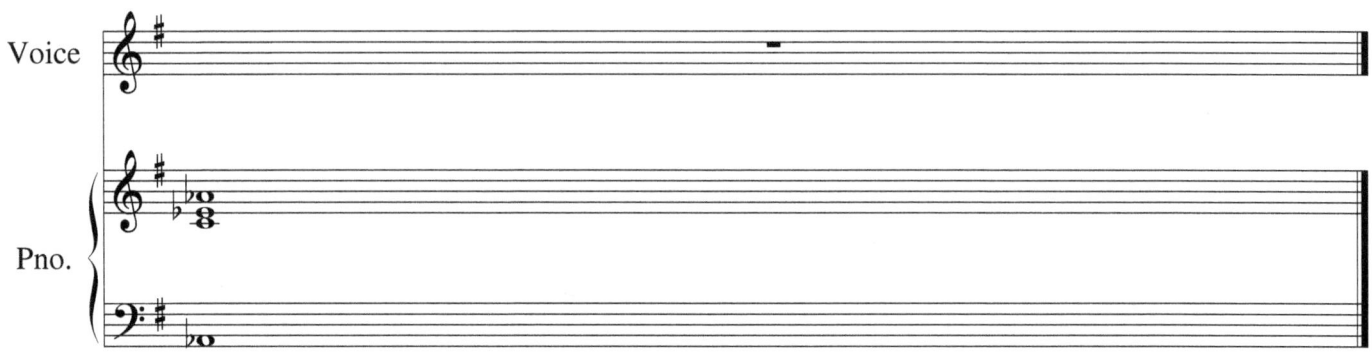

198

I Frightened Him Away

Music and Lyrics by Mel Atkey

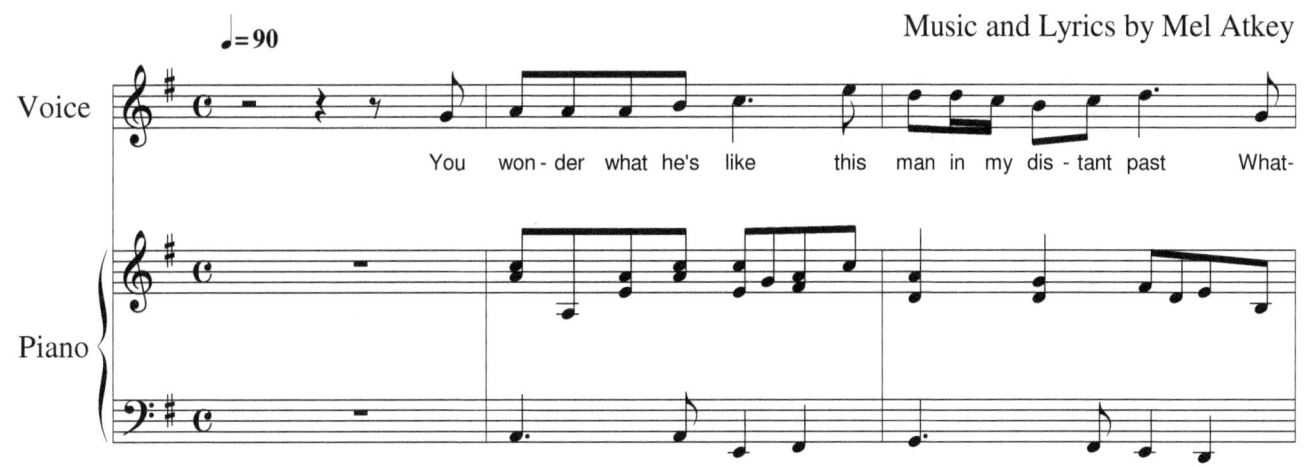
You wonder what he's like this man in my distant past What-

ever became of Mike and why it didn't last   Wistful eyes, / All aglow

carrying no great surprise, / with passion he'll never know   Painfully shy and pensive, / Keeping it all inside me   confident, strong and sensitive, / Making his berth too wide for me

© 2013 The Friendlysong Company Inc.

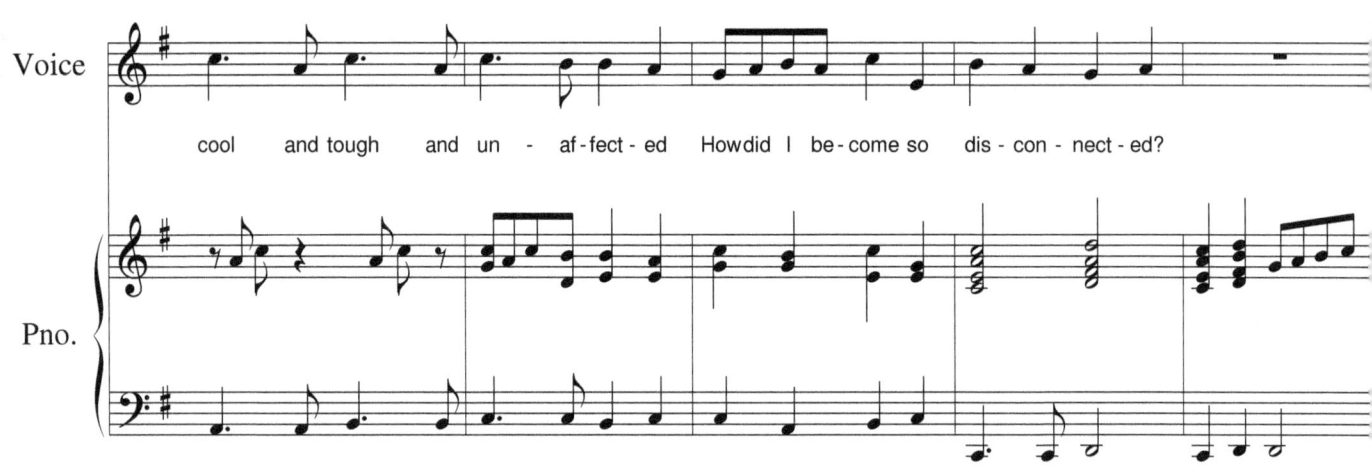

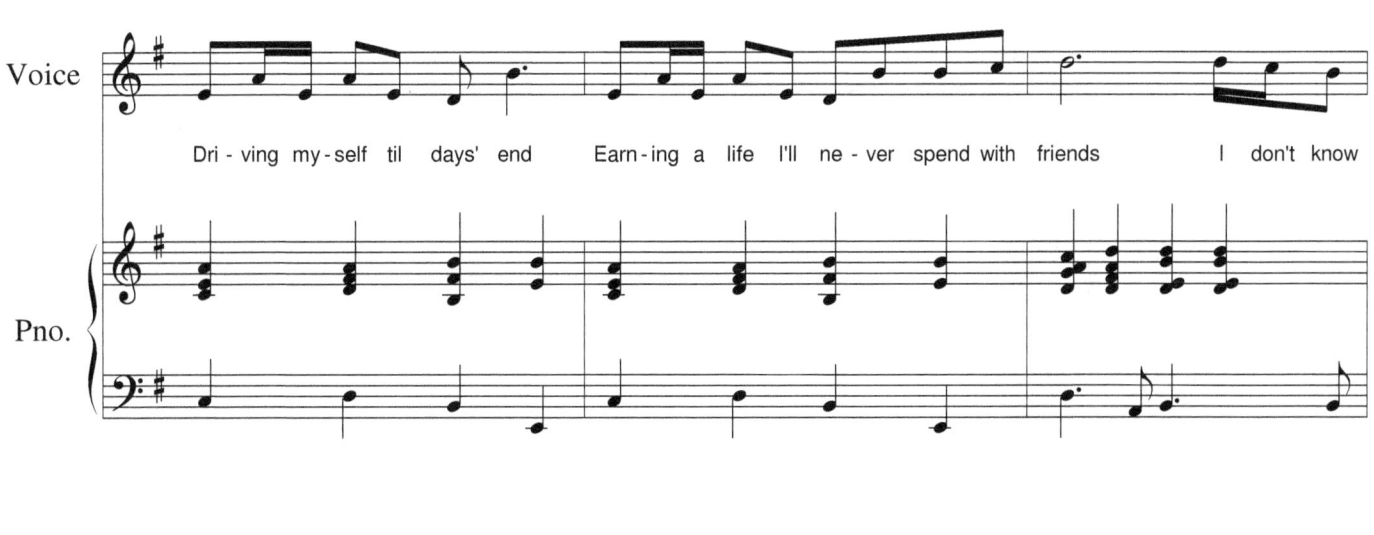

A Cold Front

© 2010 The Friendlysong Company, Inc.

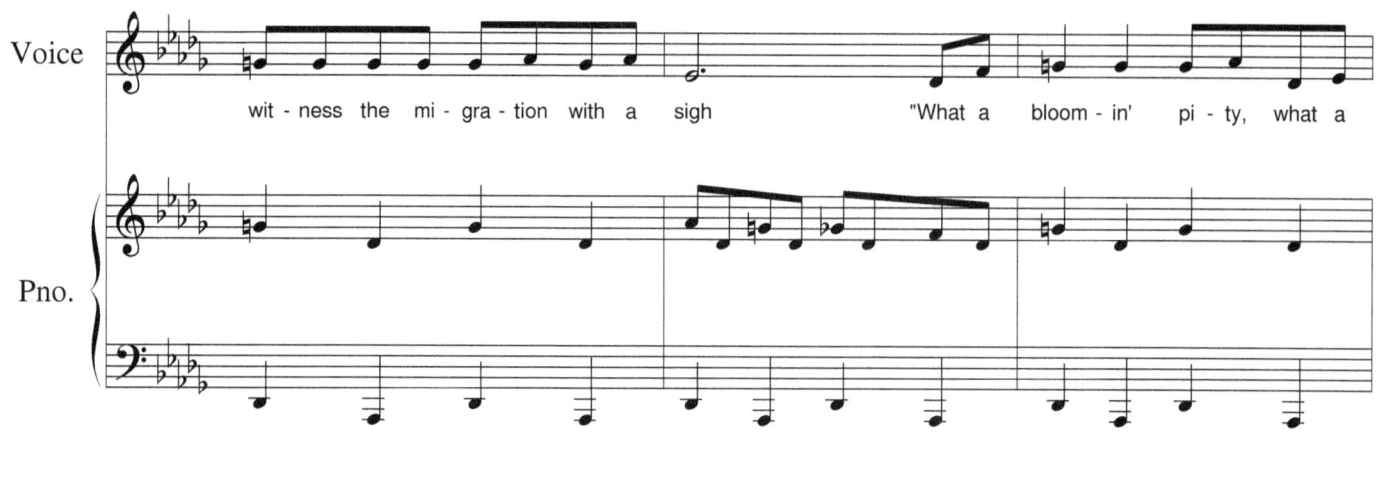
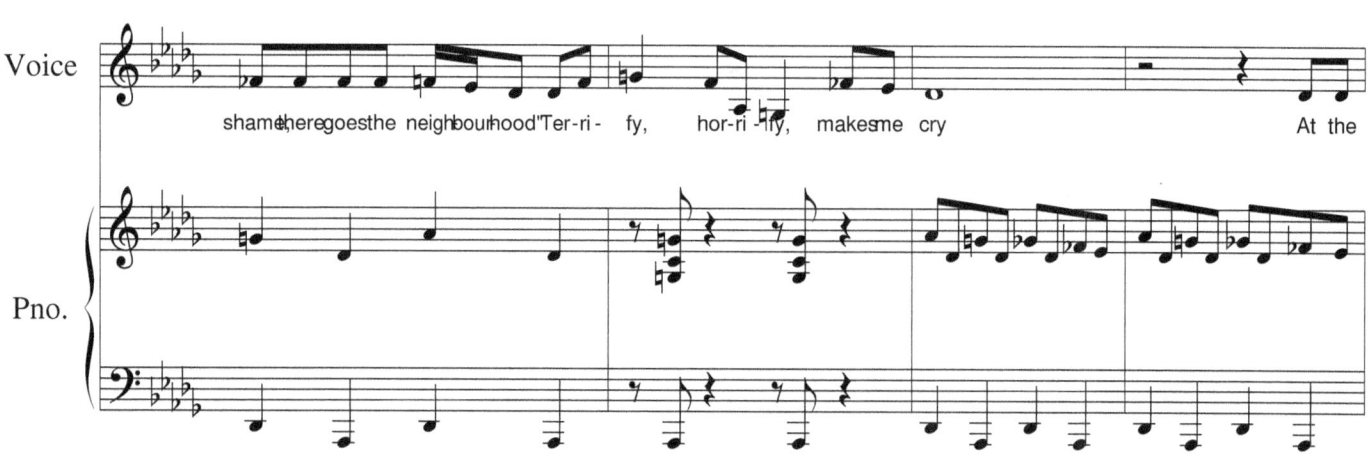

The Power of Advertising

© 2010 The Friendlysong Company, Inc.

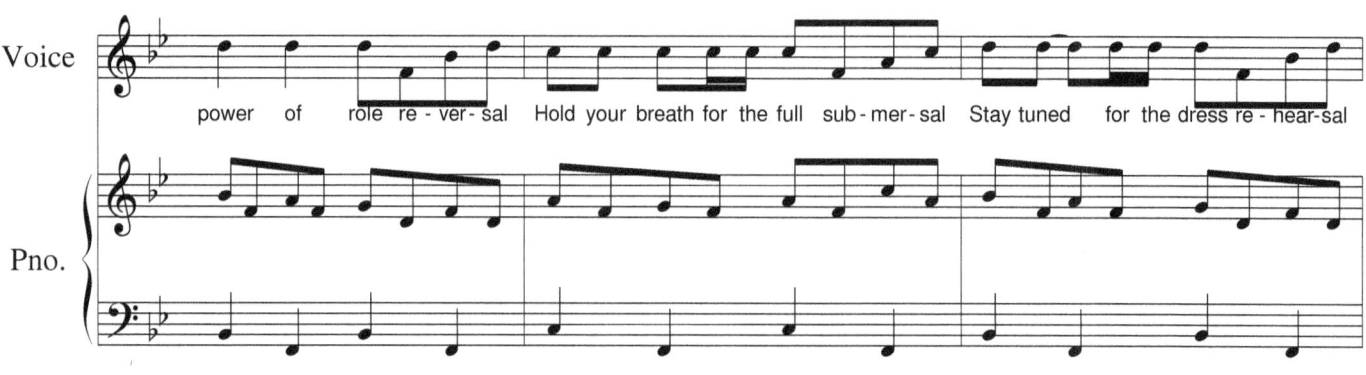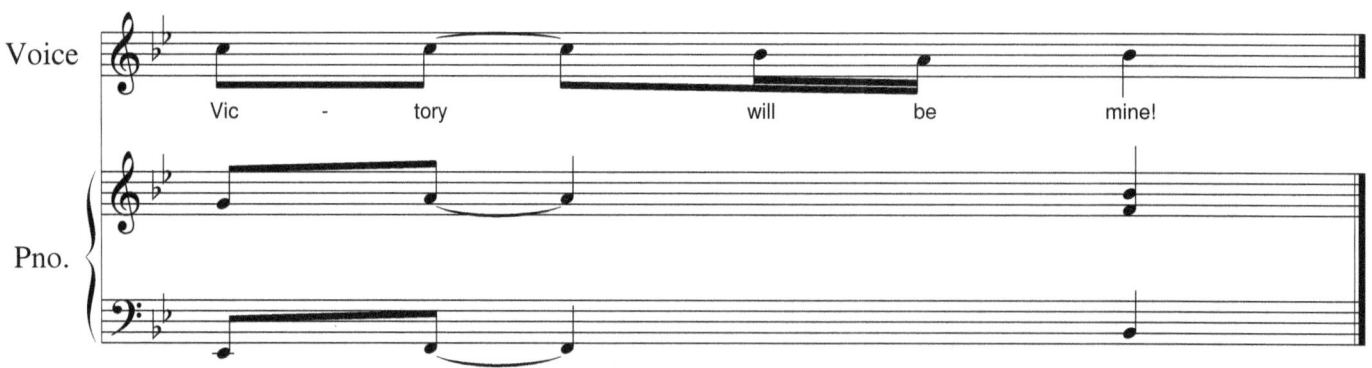

Picasso

Music and Lyrics by Mel Atkey

© 1999 The Friendlysong Company, Inc.

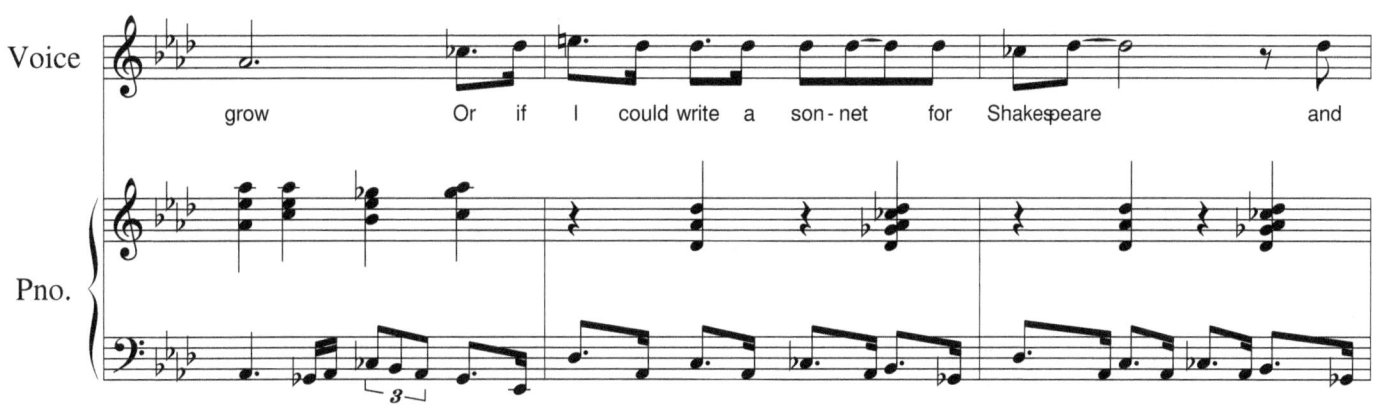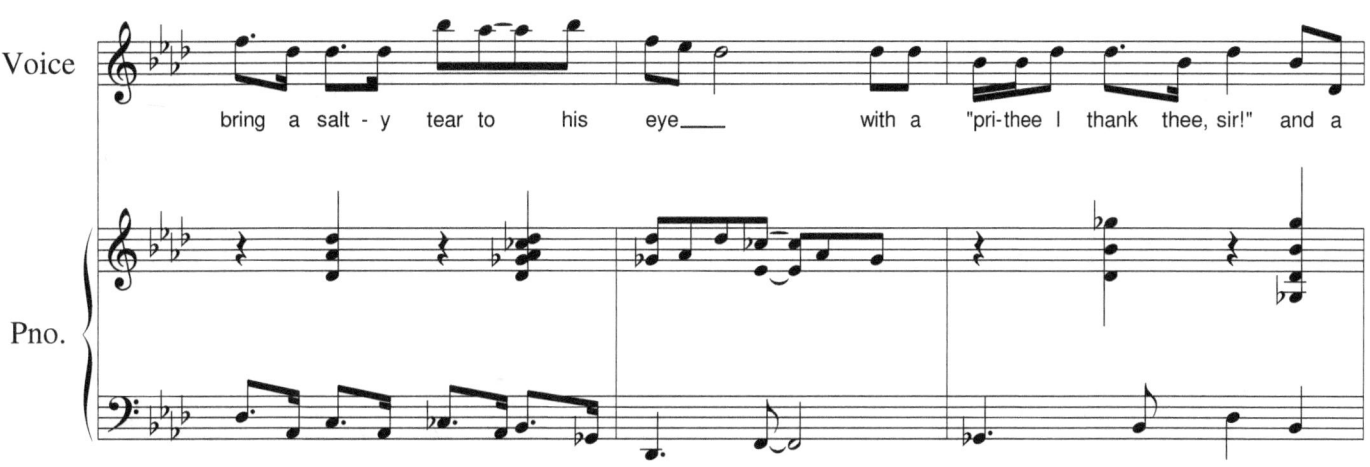

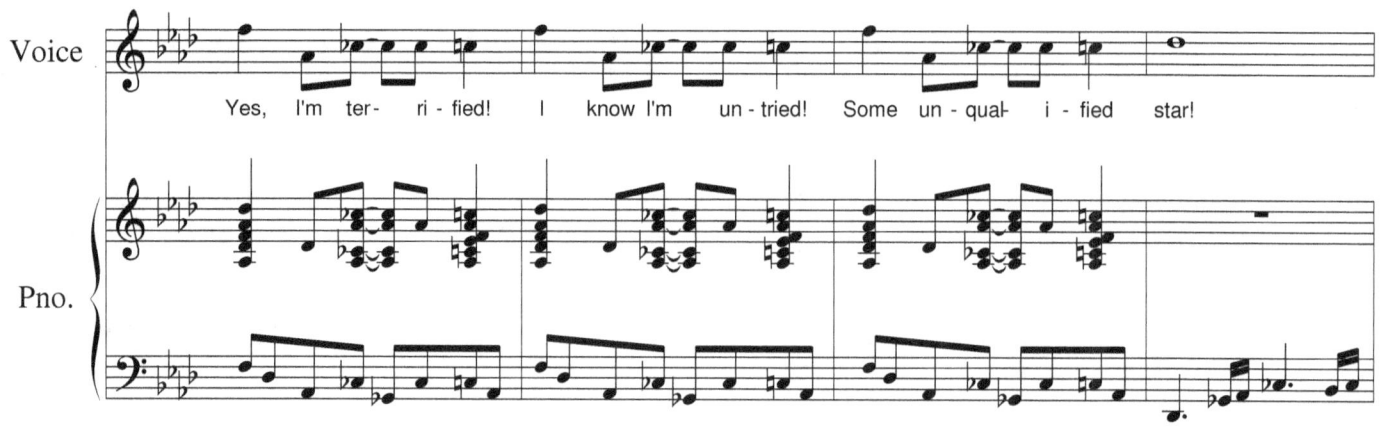

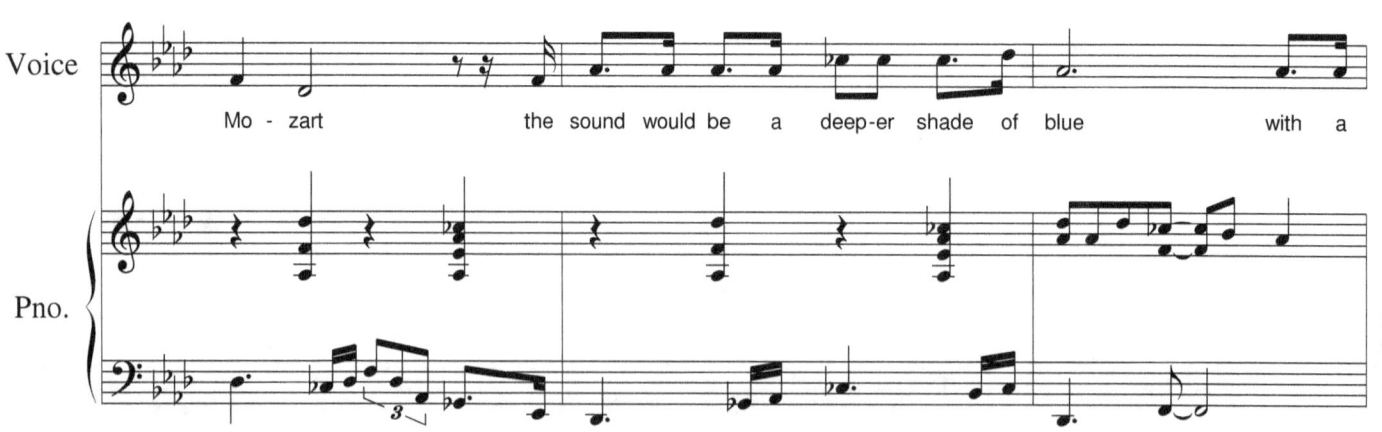

Alone on Christmas Eve

Music and lyrics by Mel Atkey

© 2013 The Friendlysong Company, Inc.

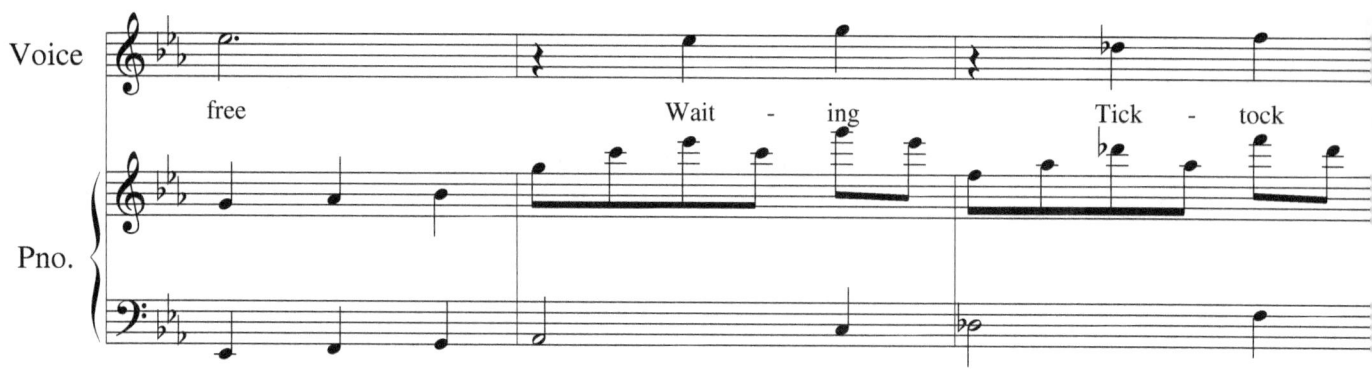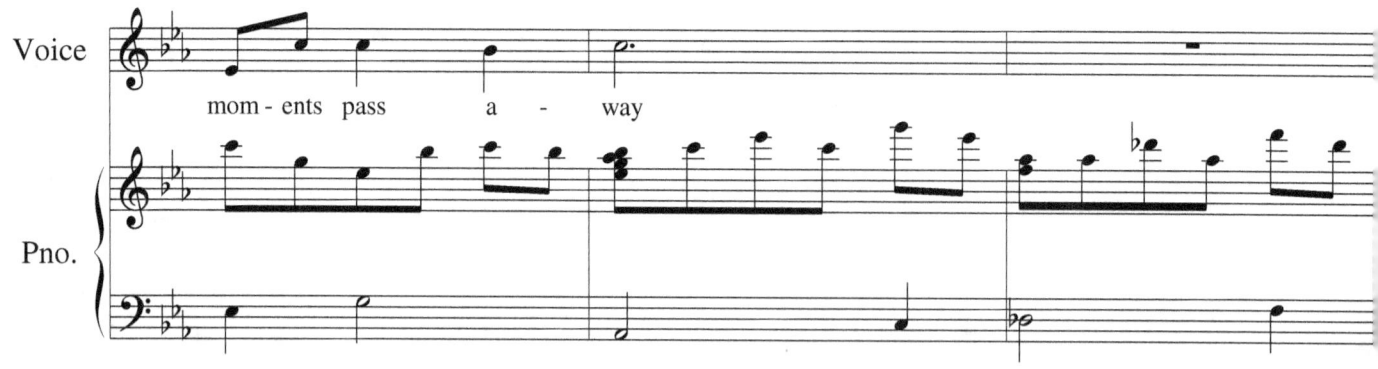

229

www.ingramcontent.com/pod-product-compliance
Lightning Source LLC
Chambersburg PA
CBHW080046230426
43672CB00014B/2829